Why can't I... Why can't I... Why can't I...
Can't I... Why can't I... Why can't I... Why
I... Why can't I... Why can't I... Why can
Why can't I... Why can't I... Why can't I...
Can't I... Why can't I... Why can't I... Why
I... Why can't I... Why can't I... Why can
Why can't I... Why can't I... Why can't I...
Can't I... Why can't I... Why can't I... Why
I... Why can't I... Why can't I... Why can
Why can't I... Why can't I... Why can't I...
Can't I... Why can't I... Why can't I... Why
I... Why can't I... Why can't I... Why can
Why can't I... Why can't I... Why can't I...

Why can't I...
fly like a superhero?

and other questions
about movement

Why can't I...
fly like a superhero?

and other questions
about movement

Sally Hewitt

Thameside Press

Distributed in the United States by
Smart Apple Media
1980 Lookout Drive
North Mankato, MN 56003

Editor: Claire Edwards
Designer: Jacqueline Palmer
Picture researcher: Diana Morris
Consultant: Anne Goldsworthy

The bicycle on pages 16–17 was photographed with the kind permission of Action Bikes, 176 High Road, Chiswick, London W4 1PR, U.K.

Printed in Hong Kong

9 8 7 6 5 4 3 2 1

Library of Congress Cataloging-in-Publication Data

Hewitt, Sally.
    Fly like a superhero? / written by Sally Hewitt.
        p. cm. -- (Why can't I)
    Includes index.
    ISBN 1-930643-03-9
      1. Motion--Miscellanea--Juvenile literature. [1. Motion--Miscellanea. 2. Science--Miscellanea. 3. Questions and answers.] I. Title. II. Series.

    QC127.4 .H47 2001
    531--dc21

                                            2001027181

Picture acknowledgements:
Brett Baunton/Stone: 12b background, 13c background.
R. Berenholtz/Stockmarket: f cover background, 10tr background.
Ed Bock/Stockmarket: 21tr. Manfred Danegger/NHPA: 8tr, 9tl, 28t, 30t.
Dimaggio/Kalish/Stockmarket: 14tr. ExtraEye: 15tr. Pictor International:
5 background, 9tr background, 23cr background. Powerstock-Zefa:
23 background. Eric Soder/NHPA: 8tl, 8ct. Zefa-Mathis/Stockmarket:
11bl background.

All other photography by Ray Moller.

Contents

Why can't I fly like a bird?   8

Why can't I fly like a superhero?   10

Why can't I float in the sky?   11

Why can't I toboggan uphill?   12

Why won't my truck move on its own?   14

Why won't my boat sail without wind?   15

Why do I have to pedal my bike?   16

Why can't I throw a balloon as far as my ball?   18

Why can't I roller skate on square wheels?   20

Why can't I slide on carpet?   21

Why can't I squash a stone?   22

Why do I leave footprints in the snow?   23

Why can't I pick up food with a magnet?   24

Movement words   26

How do you move?   27

Notes for parents and teachers   28

Index   30

Why can't I fly like a bird?

Because you don't have wings.

Birds have very light bones
and strong muscles
for flapping their wings.

Your bones are much
heavier than a bird's.

You would need
very strong wings
to lift you
off the ground
and move you
through the air.

Why can't I fly like a superhero?

Because of gravity.

Gravity is a force.
You can't see it,
but if you try to fly,
gravity will always pull you
down towards the ground.

Why can't I float in the sky?

Because you are the wrong shape.

Without a parachute to slow you down,
gravity would pull you straight to the ground.

A parachute is a good shape
for collecting air. The air
stops you falling so fast
and lets you float down safely.

Why can't I toboggan uphill?

Because gravity
will pull you
and your toboggan
downhill.

You have to push or pull
a toboggan uphill.
If you let it go, it slides back down
to the bottom of the hill again.

Why won't my truck move on its own?

Because nothing starts to move all by itself.

You need to push or pull your truck to make it start to move.

If you put your truck on a slope and let it go, gravity will pull it down the slope for you.

Why won't my boat sail without wind?

Because the wind blows into the sails and pushes the boat along.

Your boat won't start moving without a push from the wind.

Why do I have to pedal my bike?

Because a bicycle won't start to move by itself.

Pedaling is a way of pushing your bike along.

You have to pedal hard to go uphill, because gravity is pulling you downhill.

You can speed downhill without pedaling at all!

Why can't I throw a balloon...

Because a balloon
is very light.

Even if you throw
a balloon very hard,
it will soon start to sink
to the ground.

as far as my ball?

Your ball is heavier
than a balloon.
When you throw it,
it will keep going
for longer.

Why can't I roller skate on square wheels?

Because square wheels won't roll along.

Circles are the best shape for turning round and round.

You can push heavy things more easily if you put them on wheels.

Why can't I slide on carpet?

Because your feet
and the carpet
rub against each other
and slow you down.

Ice skates slide over ice
because they are
both fairly smooth
and don't rub against
each other so much.

Why can't I squash a stone?

Because a stone is very hard.

You can squash clay because it is soft.
Once you have squashed clay,
it stays in its new shape.

Why do I leave footprints in the snow?

Because you sink into the snow.

You push down on the snow harder than the snow can push up on you.

Why can't I pick up food with a magnet?

Because food is not made of iron.

Magnets can pull metal things made of iron towards them.

They can pick up things such as pins and paper clips.

If a magnet could pick up your food, the food certainly wouldn't be very good to eat!

Movement words

air You can't see air but it is all around you. Air pushes up on a parachute to slow it down as it falls.

force A force pushes or pulls on things to make them go faster or slower.

gravity Gravity is a force that pulls things towards the Earth and makes them fall down to the ground.

heavy Things that are heavy weigh a lot. Heavy is the opposite of light.

light Things that are light don't weigh very much. Light is the opposite of heavy.

magnet A magnet pulls things made of iron towards it. This force is called magnetism.

pull You can start something moving by pulling it towards you. A pull is the opposite of a push.

push You can start something moving by pushing it away from you. A push is the opposite of a pull.

squash You can squash or push a soft object made of something such as clay or sponge to change its shape.

stretch You can stretch or pull an object made of something such as clay or elastic to change its shape.

wind Wind is moving air. It can push things along.

How do you move?

Which of the words below would you use to describe the different ways you move in these everyday activities?

- Make a clay model
- Play football
- Brush your teeth
- Ride a bike
- Make your bed
- Write a letter
- Eat a meal

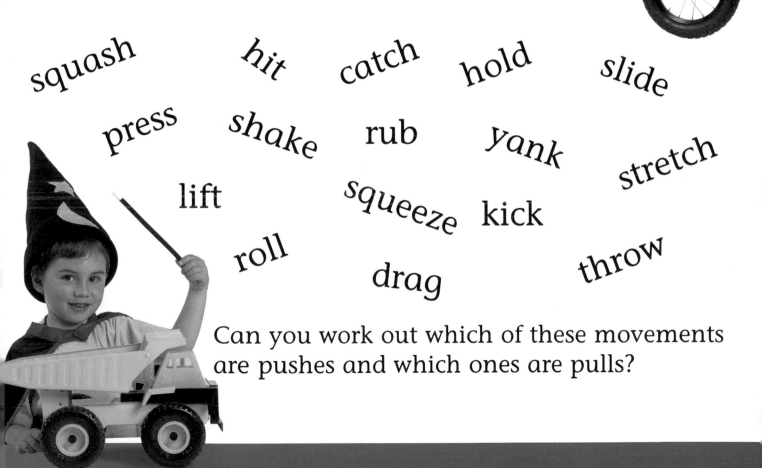

squash   hit   catch   hold   slide

press   shake   rub   yank   stretch

lift   squeeze   kick

roll   drag   throw

Can you work out which of these movements are pushes and which ones are pulls?

Think about all the things that move and what makes them move. Is there anything that never moves?

Notes for parents and teachers

Children know that they can't fly, but they may not know the reason why. Read the simple answers to the questions about movement, and then you may like to try out these activities with your child. They will help to reinforce the ideas in this book and give you plenty to discuss.

Heavy and light

Collect objects of different sizes and weights such as a balloon, an apple, and some coins. Guess which are heavy and which are light. Pick them up and talk about how they feel. Put them in order of weight. Are big things always heavier than small things?

Fill some same-size food bags with different types of food, such as potatoes, flour, or pasta. Put two bags side by side and guess which one is heavier just by looking at them. Weigh them to find out if you were right.

Movement words

Make some little apple pies together and use movement words to describe what you are doing. Talk about when you are pushing and pulling. Shake the flour and watch it fall through a sieve. Rub the fat and flour to make crumbs, then stir in a little water, push and squash the mixture into a ball, roll out the pastry, and press the pastry cutter to cut out.

Find some paper, some modeling material, a sponge, an elastic band, some cloth, and a wooden block. Notice and discuss what happens when you try to push, squash, stretch, and fold them.

Falling down

Collect objects that can be dropped without breaking—such as a wooden block, a sponge, a spoon, a paper tissue, a leaf, and a piece of paper. One by one, hold them up high and drop them. Talk about how they fall. Do they fall straight down? Does the air seem to push up on some more than others? How can you tell? Do any go up? Why not?

Experiment with using a paper plate, a large handkerchief, or some paper to make a parachute. Attach four pieces of string around the edges and tie on a small plastic toy. Which parachute works best?

Magnetism

Play with fridge magnets. Look for the little magnets at the back. Try placing the fridge magnets on different surfaces. Guess whether the magnet will be attracted to each surface.

Find a magnet and make a collection of small objects including several made of metal. Sort them into groups of the ones the magnet will pick up and those that it won't.

Index

balloon 18, 19

bicycle 16, 17

downhill 12, 16, 17

flapping 9

floating 11, 18

flying 8, 9, 10

footprints 23

gravity 10, 11, 12,
    14, 16, 26

ice-skating 21

parachute 11

pedaling 16, 17

roller-skating 21

rolling 20

rubbing 21

sliding 13, 21

squashing 22, 26

throwing 18, 19

tobogganing 12

uphill 13, 16

wheels 20

wind 15, 26

wings 8, 9